THE LITTLE HAUNTED BOOK
OF POEMS

Ginger Lee

Designed by Ginger Lee

Printed in the United States of America

ISBN 978-17350544-2-1

Author's Website: www.gleewrites.com

Without

The whole world watched
As I withered away
Without your love
I became decay
Back to the earth
My body belonged
A lost spirit floated free
Haunted and wronged

Longing

Crunching leaves and a familiar chanting murmur drifts
through barren trees
A smell of smoke and burning oak wood is carried by
the breeze
My senses perk up as I spy my other half in supplication
to the moon
Closer still I long to tend to hidden wounds
My need grows and desire builds filling every part of me
Reunited at last I cling to him as I fall onto my knees

Soon

I clenched my jaw
And heard a crow caw
The spices prepared
Filled putrid air
My beloved's silent body
Lay very still
Soon to be buried
On the highest hill
The place we were to become
One flesh and bone
Tragically now
I was alone

Marrow

I found it first
Leftover from the hunt
Discarded but meat still
Left on the bone
My mate soon arrived
He followed my scent, clever fellow
I already partook, but left him the marrow

Twitch

My bed doesn't feel like my bed
Something is off in my head
The body it lays
Weighed down
No fingertips tapping
Not one toe twitch
A scream will not be heard
Paralysis of the tongue
If I catch a breath
I'll know I'm alive
This night, I may not survive

Metal Man

Tick tick
Tick tick
Gears turn
Click click
Burning and yearning
The metal man's heart
Loved his creator
From the very start

Caged

Such a sweet bird
A rare beauty indeed
Fitting to be admired
By the king
A quiet demeanor
Under a guise
Her offerings are twisted
Fulfilling desires
Her cage, his bedchamber
But pity, she does not need
His darkness delights her
No wish to be free

It Lays

An envelope closed with a wax seal
Never opened by her delicate fingers
Gathering dust from days
Then weeks
Then months where it lays
The contents forgotten
Something she will not see
Words written on paper
Now the broken pieces of me

Cursed

To love so deeply
To feel so much
Then they leave
The pain
It cuts
Their name is left
On the tip of your tongue
Unholy thirst
An endless curse

Turned

The girl loved the wolf
The wolf loved her blood
His human form
Brought lustful delight
But he took her life
When day turned to night

You

Forlorn words
Spoken with soft lips
Uttered on the wind
Float over my final resting place
This past body of mine
Under the earth
While you stand here
Alive and taking a breath
I will find you
In the next life
My darling

A Haunting List

A haunting list
Rolled up in my clenched fist
Pull the covers up high
For you, I'm coming to spy
I promise to be nice
Just don't look at me twice

Watching

Goosebumps come
His breath
It escalates
Watching her from the woods
Shadows obnubilate
He wants it badly
But always waits
Sweet flesh too innocent
To take a taste

Mine

The lantern light glowed
Sand between my toes
Fingers intertwined
He said he would be mine
I gave him everything
Every heartbeat
Every kiss
How was I to know
This would be the last night
I was his

The Drink

I smoothed my palm
Across the crisp linen cloth
Then placed it in my lap
A woman in midnight blue
Delivered a goblet
Of smokey caliginous juice
Cool crystal kissed my lips
As I sipped then drank it down
I had ordered the most potent poison
Very soon I wouldn't be around

Side by Side

Forever dwelling
Behind iron gates
Side by side gravestones
They made perfect mates
The spirit of the boy
The spirit of the girl
Till the end of everything
To haunt and toil

My Tale

Tales only, they may be
Of bats and vampires
And creaking old houses
And I, carrying a candlestick lit
Padding up rickety steps
To meet the dark one
Waiting at the top for me

Primus

Wicked whispers all around
As he led her through the crowd
A scandalous affair indeed
Her fragile mortality intrigued
As respected primus of the brood
He made sure she did not become the food

Tipped

The witches have your name
Sliding through their lips
The rum has them dancing
And swaying iniquitous hips
The chanting grows louder
And your fate, it tips

Like a Ghost

Much like a dream
He never wanted to wake from
The evanescence of her silhouette
Lingered in his bedroom
He still smelled her perfume
On the pillowcase
But she was not here
Like a ghost
He wished would make itself known
By rattling the chandelier

Skeleton Key

A long dark corridor
Is meant to be explored
With creaking floors
And thick wooden doors
Clicking of locks
With a turn of the skeleton key
What lies behind them
Remains to be seen

The Owl

The owl's favorite spot
Perched upon a skull
Gathering up squeaking mice
Soon his belly is full
All through the night
From cranium to field he flies
Talons snatching up tiny creatures
Until the moonlight dies

Frightening

The stories told by the aged harridan
Frightened feral children of the town
Ghosts and goblins and ghastly things
Described in such grotesque and gruesome detail
Kept them from wandering out of bounds

The Attic

Wails coming from the attic
But she hasn't been
Locked up there
In so long
Maybe it's the
Horrible memories
Of all the ways
She was wronged

Look No Further

If bedlam is what you seek
Look no further
The wild things come here
To torment and tease
With scalpels and blood on their sleeves
Nightmares and dreams
For some, peace
For others, screams

One Simple Request

Numb and at rest
Eyes blink then a breath
Slow heart beating
Withing this cavernous chest
"Give me the leeches"
Just one simple request
I wish to feel something
Anything, please
Sometimes pain is best

Aware

It's not for the faint of heart
Please look away for the next part
My scalpel makes the cut
With a steady hand slicing through
I cauterize the oozing
Minimizing loss is what I do
Expert removal of disease
Finally stitching you up, perfectly neat

Now Hiring

I will offer an apprentice higher pay
For I do not keep hours during the day
They must not be easily queasy
The…job I perform
Well, it isn't easy
You see, it's in the shadows
Where dangerous demons lurk
And special skills are required for this work

A Fresh Start

The word creature
Suggests he was created
That's precisely what I've done
A perfect laboratory specimen
Starting my lover's life over
It has begun
He will cherish and remember me
From the happy times gone by
I excised very particular amygdala
In formaldehyde it now lies

Healer

Safety first
Is my motto
When you come
To me for healing
I solemnly swear
The straps are there
For your wellbeing

To Drown

You picked your poison
Now drink it down
The medicine chosen
Will help you drown
Quietly and peacefully
Slowly falling asleep
Sinking under the waves
Final rest in the deep

Anomaly

Would you give me your attention
If I was an anomaly
Beautifully odd and different
Pulling out desire uncommonly

A Tonic

Sir, I need a tonic
Not one I would normally find
I'm in search of the perfect elixir
To make the gentleman mine

A Night at the Theatre

Ether held to the nose
Take a deep breath in
A gruesome gathering
A surgical spectacle to begin
You lay in lethargy
The theatre is packed
The surgeons are ready
Quickly bestowing your femur a whack
Your eyes fly open
As the flutist's fingers flit
You'll never forget the taste
Of the leather strap you bit

The Plan

Yes, a tourniquet on every extremity
That's right
I'm losing my limbs to this illness
I planned it this way
Having them cut off
Only needing my head and my heart
All of the rest will rot and decay

A Recipe

An extract of this
A sliver of that
Dashes of spice
Pinches of bat
This brew boils
A scent so divine
Easy to swallow
Much like sweet wine
I don't blame you
For taking it all
You couldn't have known
It would bring such trauma
My secret ingredient
Is the purple belladonna

My Boy

"Mercy!" the nurse cried
As the wild-eyed bewildered doctor
Pulled the kicking screaming
Creature from my womb
Others in the suite gasped
As I, spent and sweating from labor
Sat up and reached for him, my odd boy
And a mother's love bloomed

At Midnight

This requiem I have written
Long before I've gone
Will be read by the man in the moon
Out on the starlit lawn
I wish for my ashes to be spread
Along the edge of the dark pond
Precisely at the stroke of midnight
And the mourners
Shall weep until dawn

Night Hunting

Her ears perked up
As sounds of small
Nocturnal creatures
Dotted the forest floor
And high upon limbs
The owls watched
Under moonlight
As her whiskers and nose twitched
Ready to pounce
This Machiavellian feline forager

These Places

Black as pitch
Curled up in corners
Stygian shadows
Consume
It is in these places
Where comfort cradles me
And infinite ideas
Bloom

Rotten Love

Love like a cellar
Dark and dim and cold
A creeping crawling lust
Dirty and rotten and bold
Desire and need in all forms
Forging an oddly bond
Soulmates bound forever
Into the grave and beyond

Your Shadow

With my unbelieving eyes
Your shadow passed
I watched it travel along the walls
I pulled the quilt up over my nose
Trying not to make the slightest noise
It stopped and stared at the foot of my bed
But it can't be you for you are dead

Sweet Sleep

This grave hugs me like a forgotten friend
Oh, the restful slumber I've been longing for is finally
here
A chant to call upon the rolling fog
It obliges and comes over me like a blanket
Night sounds lull me to sweet sleep
Unmatched peace is found behind the cemetery gates

Abandoned

I'm finding it hard to breathe
This thick air filled with dust
Settling over everything
Even me
The moon is out
But it is dark here
And the silence
Rings in my ears
There is nothing to see
They moved on
And left desolate walls
Where family photographs hung

www.ingramcontent.com/pod-product-compliance
Lightning Source LLC
Chambersburg PA
CBHW060529280326
41933CB00014B/3117